UNTOLD STORIES:

12 Stories of Successful American Acupuncturists in the New Millennium

BONNIE KOENIG, LAC
JASON STEIN, LAC

My Big Fat Orange Cat Publishing

Contents

Introduction

By
Bonnie Koenig LAc

Tracking down 12 successful acupuncturists talking about their success wasn't easy. Fortunately, I had Jason Stein to do the dirty work of setting up appointments while they made time in their busy schedules to talk to him about their practices. Why would we go out and do that? Certainly the appeal of reading about successful acupuncturists has a limited audience. Given the nature of the business and how scary it is to get out of school deeply in debt, it was important to highlight practitioners who built successful practices.

When I graduated from Oregon College of Oriental Medicine in 1999, we had one business class that encompassed everything from marketing to the basics of a business license. We had a practitioner who had graduated two years before with a thriving practice come chat with us about what worked for her in the area she set up. We talked about something called a 'tag line'.

What I took out of that class was to not start your office too big and to have a short pithy sentence about what I did as an acupuncturist. What I did not have, and probably needed, could fill volumes. This book focuses on the different paths practitioners have taken once they have moved past the 'not too big' stage.

Instead of taking, "Don't start with too big of an office," to mean don't *start* too big, my brain rearranged that thinking to "Don't think too big, *ever*." That became a problem which I hope to help others avoid.

It became a problem because I didn't take risks that I should have taken as soon as I could have. I played small, starting out of my home (which is great for some people, but can be harder to get started as not everyone will take a home based service business seriously). Even after having had some success out in another office, when I moved to a new area, I remained small, renting a single room with limited services rather than taking a chance that I could have had more, both for me and my patients.

The other problem with this type of thinking is the fear of growth. After all, it was hard enough to set up a business where I was a sole practitioner. Taking on employees seemed hugely complicated. Renting out rooms seemed like another headache. Ah, the stress of it. In fact, I didn't do any of that. I witnessed other practitioners struggle with it. Some, like me, decided not to do it at all. One woman made that decision but is in partnership with another practitioner who was willing to take on those additional administrative tasks. I worry that there are many others out there stagnating and getting frustrated with a business that is a success but needs to grow to keep thriving.

Business is constantly learning. There are lots of legal details that we need to stay current on and grow with.

There are many different business models and some overlap with others.

When I went into practice, most people were sole practitioners, working in their clinic alone or with an administrative person to assist. Some had other people renting rooms from them on the days they did not work. Sometimes they might have taken an office with an extra room to sublet to another practitioner on a regular basis.

Since then, there are examples of many more business models. There is the community acupuncture model which has gained popularity as a way to bring acupuncture to those who don't have insurance coverage or the money to pay for private treatments. I have seen the growth of the associate model. The associate isn't just a person who rents space, but a person who is paid by another practitioner to work as an employee.

There are people who specialize in a niche area and grow their practice by focusing on that specialty. There are others who have put their previous background to work helping other practitioners succeed in business. There are still others who have found a niche and work within that niche creating products. I am amazed that there are two practitioners in this book who work at hospitals. The idea of a hospital job was unheard of (practically speaking) in 1999. Now there are jobs advertised for hospital work as well as working for the VA.

Acupuncture as a profession has grown. That means the paths to success have multiplied. It's easy to get caught up in the stress of having loans that are overwhelming and not enough patients. It helps to remember that there are people out there creatively making a good living. Certainly these paths are not for everyone. I don't mean to imply that everyone can get there, but these people did. That means it's possible.

I struggled my entire acupuncture career. I had months of success and a lot of months of stress. I helped a lot of people. Then I lost a very good deal on a room and I sat back and decided I wanted to write instead. I was already writing daily with two blogs that I kept up. I was starting to guest blog for pay. I liked being able to just write. For me there was a joy in even the waiting times, wondering if I would get some money, that hadn't ever existed in the down times of acupuncture. I finally began to think that I was more suited to writing.

My failures to thrive as an acupuncturist taught me a lot about business. I go back to that idea of don't start too big and rethink it. Yeah, don't start too big but don't limit yourself to being too small. You have to think big enough to not just pay the bills but to allow yourself to take vacations and to thrive and grow. If you're not doing that, your business isn't supporting you like it should. Think of ways you can allow it to grow big enough to take care of you. Think of it being bigger than it 'must' be to pay your monthly bills. That allows it to get to a place where you can pay the bills and not be worried about the following month.

Have a plan. Be willing to revise the plan. I believe it's Alyssa Johnson who talks about starting over three times with a different practice. The first practice wasn't busy enough for her. The second was too busy. She has hopes that this third incarnation is just right. Johnson isn't afraid to rebrand herself and reinvent the business to serve her as well as the people around her. Our lives and our needs change.

I started out in a home based business and it wasn't the right choice. Other practitioners have built a business outside their home and then moved it into their home and have done well. That works for them. Their needs changed from needing to be out in the world to work to just wanting to serve and keep costs down. One practitioner even searched for the perfect house so she could work out of her home. After two years she found a home that worked. Finding what you want can take time.

One thread that runs through all these practitioner stories is that each of them struggled. They each had to overcome obstacles and fears. Many were ready to quit, sometimes more than once. But they all made the decision to keep trying. They all ended up being successful because of that. Be realistic about the timing. Building a business takes time. Be realistic about what works for you. The more you know yourself, the quicker you'll know if a situation will suit you or not.

Don't be afraid of trying something. Yes, you might spend money and you might fail. You might fail spectacularly but you may also succeed. Understand what is calling to you and try and follow that path. Remember the successful path isn't always straight. It may mean trying different business models or rebranding yourself a few times before you get to where you need to be. There's nothing wrong with trying and learning something.

Use down time to focus on what you really want and what you really need. Focus on those things you can change. Do you like a certain type of patient? Then find out where those patients hang out. Are you detail oriented and want to learn everything that you can about a particular subject? You might think about whether a specialization could be for you. Do you like variety and being busy? Running a community clinic might be for you. Or maybe you want to be a clinic manager with several other practitioners working for you.

There is no one path for success. If you're like me and tend to flit from one thing to another, you may find that after a decade or so of working you need something else. Maybe you create an amazing product that fills a need not currently being met. You may even find a niche that no one has even considered. But that's up to you.

This book is to remind you that it's okay to think big. It's okay to think about thriving. Thriving as an acupuncturist will take work. Lots of it, but it can be done. I wanted to show you some examples of people who made it so you can hold them up as models. As acupuncturists we have far more models of people just barely paying the rent than those of practitioners who are really successful.

Let's celebrate the success even as you work towards your own.

Bonnie Koenig, LAc
    Author at My Big Fat Orange Cat Publishing

Welcome

by
Jason Stein, LAc

Having been a witness to the road that hundreds of student's traverse on their journey from school into practice, including my own, I have seen one undeniable commonality: The theory and practice of Chinese Medicine has impacted each of us in such a profound way that we have willingly taken on the mental, physical and economic challenge that becoming a part of this profession entails. The power of this medicine has led us all down a career path filled with a myriad of obstacles, such as insurance, loan repayment, and even mainstream acceptance of the medicine itself. But why?

For each of us this answer is slightly different. Perhaps, like me, your trajectory from some other profession to Chinese Medicine changed when, despite your invincible exterior, an illness knocked you off the path. You went through the invasive diagnostics only to hear the words, "unknown origin", or perhaps you were labeled with a chronic disease. The ultimate course of your treatment often follows the same path of options: drugs, surgery, or 'there's nothing we can do'. And, then came along your knight in shining armor, or more accurately your needles in plastic casing, to revitalize your qi, rebalance your meridians, and ultimately restore your health and wellbeing.

From my own course of studying, to practicing in a hospital, and finally entering the teaching sphere the trends have become clear: Western Medicine is in need of our help. We spend more money, a lot more, on healthcare than any developed country in the world. But, to what end? As of 2014 the average American's life expectancy was rated thirty-fourth in comparison to other developed countries, landing us right between Qatar and Cuba.

Why is the healthcare system in the US on the brink of collapse?

To start, insurance premiums raise an average of 10% per year, with the baby boomers becoming elderly, we are headed for a nursing shortage, and more and more doctors are leaving the field to enter another profession, retirement, or, far too often by taking their own lives – at a staggering average of one suicide every day. Western Medicine has become more focused on the bottom line than on the health and well-being of its patients. It is this greed that has forced America's healthcare system to the brink of collapse.

What is the solution?

Having withstood the test of time for over 3,000 years, Chinese Medicine is an integral part of the solution. Visit any big city in the US and you will find a Chinatown, filled with calligraphy, gardens, and yes, the medicine-- a medicine founded on the betterment of the individual, as opposed to the betterment of practitioners' pocketbooks.

With institutions such as the World Health Organization, the NBA, and Oprah garnering support for Chinese Medicine, its notoriety and visibility are on a steady incline.

With this trend I have also seen an increase in the study and licensing of the medicine, unfortunately, this has come with an even greater increase in the cost of tuition.

The challenge, as I see it, is one of creating sustainable hope. We know the medicine works, but only when the practitioner is able to maintain their own health and sanity. I've witnessed many brilliant student's lights die out as they get caught up in political red tape and bureaucracy. I've watched acupuncture graduates begin businesses under-resourced and overwhelmed by the vast land of entrepreneurship. It is in this space that hope is easily lost, the hope that Chinese Medicine can be a viable part of the American healthcare solution.

So, how do we create sustainable hope?

By talking, interviewing, and exploring with the unknown heroes of our medicine --not the big name acupuncture Super Stars that walk the seminar circuit, but the individuals you may never have heard of that are making great strides in changing the way medicine looks in our backyard.

I believe in our medicine. I believe learning from the unsung heroes will allow us all to take a step forward in creating something great, whether that be making a product, teaching others how to succeed, branching out and using the medicine in a new domain such as veterinary care, or in private practice.

I invite you to watch the videos, or read the transcripts included here to replenish your hope, and remind yourself of why you stepped onto this path in the first place.

Lastly, I'd like to offer deep appreciation to Bonnie

Koenig, without whom this vision would not have come into existence.

Come join us as we listen, watch, and remember - Together is better.

Jason Stein, LAc
Chair of Professional Development, Oregon College of Oriental Medicine

PART I

The Business Owner

First and foremost, after being an acupuncturist, the practitioner must learn to be a business owner. Andy Rosenfarb, Brad Whisnant and Jill Blakeway are all excellent business owners with thriving practices. Each of them brings something unique to their practice and you'll see that they all have a different style and their practices are all run very differently.

Rosenfarb and Blakeway are specialists, although Blakeway's specialty in women's health is much more general than Rosenfarb's eye care.

Whisnant is a very busy generalist who offers some good advice to new practitioners.

The Specialist

Andy Rosenfarb, LAc graduated from Pacific College of Oriental Medicine. He is the founder and clinical director of Acupuncture Health Associates in Westfield, NJ.

Andy Rosenfarb, LAc: Planning and Persistence

Andy Rosenfarb, Licensed Acupuncturist, talks very much like he plans. There are no extraneous words, every word conveys an idea. Planning. Persistence. Then the smile. Have fun.

Rosenfarb discovered acupuncture school when he was an undergraduate studying pre-med. His father went to an acupuncturist for his health problems and after six months he was doing much better and off medications. Excited, Rosenfarb's father took his son to see his acupuncturist.

After talking to the practitioner, having a treatment, and deciding to read *The Web that Has No Weaver*, Rosenfarb says, "For me it was just like YES! This is what I'm doing...It was one of those aha moments...like the whole concept...the whole philosophy, just everything clicked right there. And I was like ah! I'm going to acupuncture school now."

Rosenfarb now runs a very busy practice in New Jersey specializing in vision care. He's gotten so busy that he took on an associate to treat fertility issues, which take up a lot of time. It's an area he no longer focuses on. Getting there took, as he re-iterates, persistence, and, of course, planning.

The first year was a struggle. He worked with four different practitioners six or seven days a week, learning the medicine, learning about business, and how to build a practice. He worked in a number of different environments. He definitely went into those positions with the intention to learn the business side of practicing. Rosenfarb says that might not be for everyone. Someone else might have the intention to learn more about a specific clinical skill or just improve their general clinical skills. No matter what the intention, working with a more experienced practitioner pays off.

Rosenfarb recalls his first year and his learning process. "Find someone who is doing what you want to do and hang out with them." He never really thought that he wouldn't make a career out of acupuncture. It was his job. "Eventually I'll make it," was Rosenfarb's underlying belief.

Rosenfarb sampled things to find out what worked for him. That's his advice to new practitioners. Sample different styles, different clinical set ups, from private practice to community to hospital settings. Follow practitioners doing things that are of interest. Work with those practitioners. While most students believe there are no jobs, jobs can be found with persistence. Rosenfarb made at least fifty phone calls to get leads on the four jobs he got in his first year.

"If a door closes, open another one," Rosenfarb says, talking about the persistence required to find people to work with.

While planning was important to Rosenfarb's success, he wasn't afraid to change his plans. Initially he'd gotten a great deal of relief from his allergies with acupuncture and he had intended to specialize in allergy relief. So although he always had a desire to specialize, vision was something he started working with after beginning his practice.

"I just woke up and I'm the eye guy now," Rosenfarb says. He works with a lot of different systems and keeps what works for him and lets go of what doesn't.

"If you specialize, you need to know it's a high level of commitment," Rosenfarb says. "You have to be the best of the best." He's not just talking about in terms of Chinese medicine but also in understanding the western medical mechanisms behind the chosen specialty. A specialist needs to understand it all. That's a big commitment.

Rosenfarb uses lists for making sure he stays committed. He sets goals for the day, the year, three years, five years and ten years. It works for him. While learning a system to keep him on task is important, he said it is more important to find a system that helps him get back on task when life interrupts. It helps him focus and design the life he wants to live, having a healthy balance between non-work time and work time.

Balancing work and life has to be an issue when you see 180 to 250 patients a week. Many of Rosenfarb's patients come in for an intensive course of treatment twice a day for one or two weeks. He works Monday through Friday.

When not treating patients, Rosenfarb is also doing research on retinitis pigmentosa, a form of genetic night blindness. He'll soon be overseeing a second phase study. The first phase was published last year with Johns Hopkins University. This second study will be a one year study funded by the National Institutes of Health.

While many acupuncturists might think Rosenfarb's clinic and research an ideal sort of endgame, he's still planning on expanding and changing his practice. He'd love to find a retinal specialist, ophthalmologist, or optometrist to work with in an integrated setting, bringing the best of both medicines to patients. He'd love to find someone with a similar vision.

"Don't take it so seriously. Have fun with it." Rosenfarb admits that he didn't know how successful he was going to be but he wanted to have fun trying. Learning from people, meeting people, and networking were all big parts of what Rosenfarb did when he created the career of his dreams.

Andy Rosenfarb, LAc can be found at **Acuvisiontherapy.com**. He's more than happy to answer questions people may have about vision issues and acupuncture.

The Generalist

Brad Whisnant is a 2007 graduate of Oregon College of Oriental Medicine. He also has a doctorate from Emperor's College where he graduated in 2011. He practices at Pin Point Acupuncture in Oregon.

Brad Whisnant: You Can't Quit

B rad Whisnant doesn't carry the excitable energy of many of the other practitioners interviewed. Whisnant waits for questions, energy controlled, but once he's asked for information passion comes out. Words tumble from his mouth when he tries to explain an experience. Everything about his manner yells strong and enduring. It shouldn't be a surprise that for Whisnant one of the key elements of success was just not quitting.

Whisnant graduated from Oregon College of Oriental Medicine in 2007 and got his DAOM from Emperor's College in 2011. "I've always wanted to help people," he says when asked how he got into the medicine. He was in the Marines and looked at many forms of serving people. Medicine seemed a positive way to go about being of service.

The focus of Whisnant's practice is on serving people and helping people feel better. He says that being of service is the key to being a success. When it came to health and healing, Whisnant knew he was the sort of person who had to get at the core of a problem. The idea of just giving someone a pill to cover up the underlying condition didn't sit well. Ultimately that was a main reason why acupuncture appealed to him.

That first year was very difficult for Whisnant. He needed to know who he was, how he wanted to practice, where he wanted to practice. "I think the bottom line... anyone being an entrepreneur, you just can't ever quit." At some point the practitioner gets to that sweet spot. It's the niche they need to fill as a healer but it only happens if the healer keeps working and doesn't give up.

At one point Whisnant was doing many different things and struggling. He was running one clinic in Oregon, one in Washington, doing house calls, and had an herbal van. He was still barely making it. The struggle was so great that he started looking at other career options. As he sat in the airport on the way to an interview, he thought about the fact that this point of capitulation was often when things turned around. Realizing he was at that point, where he was ready to quit, made him decide that quitting wasn't what he wanted at all.

"Things are so bad...it's darkest before it gets light... stay focused and keep going...and that's where it shifted," Whisnant says about his thought process during that dark time.

The last several years he's made between $300,000 and $450,000 annually. His advice is to realize that there are sick people everywhere. It doesn't matter what sort of medicine you do, you can help.

Whisnant says he was seeing up to 150 people a week, but now only sees about 100 to 120 people a week because 150 was just too many. He sees three or four people an hour. He makes a big point of referring out to others and talking to people about what sorts of medical options they have. People trust him to be honest.

He's also started a company for a cold and flu remedy. Although he has this other company, currently he's focused mostly on the clinic. He created the remedy because it was a niche area that didn't have a good product he could use to help his patients.

When asked what people need to do to create their own products, Whisnant says that it was just time, money, and, of course, not quitting. There were hoops to jump through but it wasn't hard. "Anybody can do it." Whisnant clearly brushes off his success as being special only in that he was willing to work hard to achieve it.

When asked about his advice to new practitioners, Whisnant says, "Spread out a bit and go places where there isn't so much acupuncture and Chinese Medicine." He believes that going to underserved areas will really help. While many practitioners tend to focus on the coastal areas, the Midwest has the majority of Integrative Hospitals. As people move to more underserved areas, they can get the message out in a place where they are 'the only game in town'.

"The whole world is out there for us," Whisnant continues. When he heard from four patients that there was no one in their area, he decided that if he was really trying to serve patients, he needed to be where they were. Since moving, he's been very successful.

"You need to look for about one acupuncturist to 9,000 people," he says. He really thinks that just about anyone can be successful at that ratio of potential patients to practitioners.

He mostly uses word of mouth for marketing. While he has a good web presence, he says that that's not as important to him. Most people only go to the web when they don't have a friend who will refer them to their practitioner. People ask their friends for referrals first. If you don't have that word of mouth yet, a web presence helps. Talking to people, giving talks out there, and interacting with people is the best advice he can give.

As far as what's next, Whisnant would like to write books, develop more products, or perhaps have multiple clinics. "Part of the new success is not getting so big," Whisnant says. He talks about being a waiter and pointing out that you can do really well with a certain number of tables, but if you get too busy and take on too many tables, the service goes down. You just can't handle that much. At this point, he's comfortable with the amount of work he's doing. He's not sure he wants to get bigger. It might be better to change things up, rather than growing.

Whisnant's advice to new practitioners is to get away from other practitioners, finding a place with a good ratio of people and practitioners and really putting in the long hours, and the hard work to be a success. He also advises not listening to the negative talk that you can only make $30,000 a year. "Letting go of some of the beliefs that we are taught…you can be anything you want to be," he says.

Whisnant can be contacted via the contact form on his website, **StHelensAcupuncturist.com**. He also has of seminars on **elotus.com**. He says he got a lot of help starting out and he's very happy to help the newer practitioners out there. "We can heal the world. We just need to get out there and do it."

The Specialist

Acupuncturist, author, and teacher Jill Blakeway runs the YinOva Center in New York. She also teaches at Pacific College of Oriental Medicine in San Diego.

Jill Blakeway: An Expression of Your Heart

Everything about Jill Blakeway is professional from her well coifed hair to the blue jewel tones of her dress. She presents well and speaks clearly. It's not a surprise that she runs Yin Ova, a large acupuncture clinic in New York. Blakeway has been on any number of television shows, including Dr. Oz and Martha Stewart promoting acupuncture.

Acupuncture was a second career for Blakeway. "I think of myself as old now," she says referring to the newer practitioners coming in who begin studying the medicine right after college.

"I moved to America…I'm English you can tell," Blakeway laughs. Her voice has the lovely modulation of British English when she speaks and herbs have the pronounced "h" when she talks about them. "I had had interstitial cystitis for a year…and finally I called my GP back in England," she says. His response was that he sends all his patients to an acupuncturist.

Blakeway found an acupuncturist and in two weeks she was much better. After that, she had to find out all that she could about this medicine. She gave up her career in business and went to acupuncture school. She never looked back.

Blakeway never really intended to specialize. However, the niche of women's health was what she was good at. She helped women and they referred other women with the same issues. These days Yin Ova has eleven acupuncturists so they do far more than just women's health. Different practitioners do different things. Blakeway was always good at gynecology and obstetrics and that's what people talked to her about.

She still considers herself a generalist. "This is a holistic medicine," she says. She treats what comes through the door. It just happened that the people talking about her were women who had gotten help for women's health issues. As she started seeing more people with those problems, she got even better and word spread. Even as large as her clinic is, Blakeway still relies on word of mouth for advertising.

In addition to the eleven acupuncturists, Yin Ova has a staff and a team of holistic practitioners, including, among others, a naturopath and a Pilates teacher. They team treat patients because they've been together in the clinic for years. They like and trust each other as practitioners, which, Blakeway says, is very important if you're going to work together.

"It was very scary...I didn't have much money...I was a single mom..." Blakeway remembers. She followed the man she would eventually marry to New York. She started by renting a room from another practitioner, working during times that weren't very lucrative. Of course, she did have another job while she was building her practice. It grew by word of mouth. After about a year or year and half, she rented her own little office and did everything herself.

"It was just me and the patients," Blakeway remembers fondly.

"I never doubted the medicine," Blakeway says. According to Blakeway, her early days were fun. Then she got busy enough to hire staff but she couldn't really support that. She didn't know how to create infrastructure to support a big practice. She struggled through that growing phase for a year or two. She also went through a phase when she was seeing too many patients, perhaps 100 a week, just to support the overhead.

"You do know you can have a waiting list, don't you?" Blakeway's doctor asked her. That helped her stress level a lot. Looking back, she can see where there were so many little things that she could have done, but it never occurred to her. As far as getting help, Blakeway said she did everything just a little too late.

After the waiting list, she realized she could pay other people to see the people she couldn't see. At the time, she hired independent contractors, but now her acupuncturists are all employees.

"I was very singled minded about doing this." Blakeway was lucky to have a partner who was willing to shoulder at least half the work at home. It wasn't until she got large and recruited a great team that she was able to let go of some of the work load.

"I was fearful too. I'm a cautious person," Blakeway adds. The Yin Ova Clinic expanded slowly so she didn't have to take loans. Some caution is good, she says. Practitioners shouldn't let fear paralyze them. "I do see that in some acupuncturists."

Blakeway continues, "It's very important to remember that you are in the service industry…and I try very hard to be of service." Her family works at the clinic in various capacities. They try to communicate that love and family vibe to their patients. They put care into each interaction with every patient. Everyone works to make the Yin Ova experience a calm, relaxed one for each person who walks through the door. This makes for great word of mouth and keeps the practice flourishing.

"It's really an expression of your heart," Blakeway says.

Blakeway isn't certain what's next. She has a couple of books out and is thinking about writing another one. She primarily writes books for lay people. She has been teaching a little. That's her way to give back to the profession. Currently the Yin Ova Center is full, so they will probably be expanding, but Blakeway laughs, "These days that doesn't involve me as much as it used to!"

Another change is that Blakeway is conscious of taking care of herself as well as working. Early on everything felt like a crisis. Now, she says, she's seen a lot so that there isn't much that surprises her. She's been able to work through a number of business setbacks. They seemed very huge and scary but in hindsight, they really weren't that important in the long run.

"It doesn't matter. It's all just noise," she says. She feels as if her practice really forced her to grow up.

Jill Blakeway can be found at **YinOvaCenter.com**. There's a press page and bios. She's also very active on Facebook as Jill Blakeway. The Yin Ova Center has a Facebook page but Blakeway doesn't run that page herself.

PART II

The Integrator

Alyssa H. Johnson and Sara Bublitz both work in hospital settings, integrating Traditional Chinese Medicine within the western framework. Both women love the opportunity to bring acupuncture into the world of mainstream medicine.

Johnson and Bublitz work in different hospitals in different parts of the country. In both cases, the hospital staff is interested in learning what they can about acupuncture. Both women spend a lot of time educating, not just clients, but nurses and families of clients.

They talk about the unique challenges and opportunities for practitioners interested in working in this integrated medical setting.

Hospital Internist

Alyssa H. Johnson started an integrated medicine program at Primary Children's Hospital. In 2015 she went back to study more about integrated medicine at Duke University.

Alyssa H. Johnson: Persistent and Passionate

Alyssa H. Johnson, LAc has a story like every other acupuncturist. She got very sick and turned to natural medicine, which was familiar to her because her parents used it. During this time, she tried acupuncture. Johnson says it was like coming full circle.

"Oriental medicine was what resonated best with my philosophy...what I believed the truths to really be," Johnson says. Her enthusiasm is obvious when she talks. She talks fast, words tumbling out. The word 'really' peppers her expressions. She's really happy to be doing the work she does, both for acupuncture patients and for new (or not so new) acupuncture practitioners.

Johnson's journey as a new practitioner was difficult. She started out in a new state and newly married. She had no friends or contacts in the area. On the positive side, Johnson says, she could define who she wanted to be as a practitioner. However, even as enthusiastic as positive as she is, Johnson doesn't minimize the challenges. Like Goldilocks, it took Johnson three tries to find out what she wanted. Each attempt was a very different type of practice.

She had a private practice but was seeing only one person an hour, renting a room. That didn't keep her busy enough. After that, she tried community style practice. The activity appealed to her. While Johnson had gotten almost bored with the private practice model and enjoyed the activity of the community acupuncture model, she found herself less and less able to study and improve her skills based on the types of diseases she saw. She was busy being present and reacting to the patient in front of her, rather than studying and researching how each of her treatments could be improved. After a time, that type of practice no longer resonated.

When Johnson got the opportunity to start an integrative medicine department at Primary Children's Hospital, she jumped at the chance. She never considered working in a hospital or working with kids, but the opportunity has worked well for her.

During the struggles of her first year of practice, Johnson fell back on her passion for teaching people. She worked on clarifying what she needed and wanted and where her skills were strongest. She worked on her personal development in business and in the areas she was weakest at as a practitioner and communicator.

Before starting acupuncture school, Johnson worked in a high volume chiropractic clinic. It was a huge help to be exposed to the sorts of marketing companies and opportunities available to the chiropractic field. Her general understanding of running a small healthcare business was invaluable. She wanted to teach this information and began giving classes while still in school.

"It took me a while to understand that I didn't have to have a super successful clinic to know that I could help people," Johnson said. She says she works with people on their own ideal practice rather than having a model for other acupuncturists to emulate. Johnson teaches that it's about finding your place in the medicine, not having the largest clinic around.

"We are making more jobs," Johnson continues. She took the position at the hospital because the more people who take those jobs and do them well, the more other hospitals will seek to emulate successful programs. However, right now, acupuncture is a profession where practitioners have to create their own job. Johnson says practitioners need to consider why they got into the medicine and advocate for themselves.

Johnson got the job at the hospital because she was looking for a change. Utah seemed interesting. She sent a bunch of letters of introduction and talked about what she was looking for, along with her resume. One of those letters landed on the desk of an integrative medical doctor at Primary Children's. It was the same day the doctor had gotten approval to hire an acupuncturist. Johnson never would have gotten the position without sending out those letters.

At the hospital, Johnson spends a lot of time educating the nurses. She advocates for her department. She lets nurses watch sessions and shares results. Patients, she says, come and go. Nurses stay. This is where she markets her practice. At some point, she'd like to go out and start talking with pediatricians about how acupuncture can help them.

Johnson also hopes to be able to teach the nurses how to do abdominal massage to assist with constipation. So many of the patients in the hospital have constipation and simple things that allow nurses to mitigate it without another medication is really important.

In the outpatient clinic, patients pay on their own. The hospital makes it affordable. With the inpatient clinic, the hospital will bill the insurance. If the carrier doesn't pay, the hospital works with the patient's family in setting up fees. A lot of the acupuncture treatments get gifted to the families. This is a sticking point for the hospital because there's no financial gain in having an acupuncturist. Still, patients and their families love it. The results are great but the hospital isn't currently able to make it a viable service.

In the next year, Johnson hopes that their program will grow large enough to hire another practitioner. This summer she starts a research study as well.

Johnson measures her success when the product sells and when the people get results. For practitioners, it's when clients return and communicate that they got results. It's less about the amount of people she sees or the money she makes.

In her coaching business, *I Practice Smart*, Johnson does independent career coaching. Her coaching includes one on one phone calls to help people through a specific part of their journey. This might mean a practitioner is working on hiring their first employee or working with a designer redoing a logo or tagline. Johnson is in the process of pulling together a comprehensive business start-up program.

Of course, a big part of her business is working with people who don't like marketing. Johnson says that most people who say that don't really understand marketing, or perhaps they know a piece of marketing strategy that just doesn't fit with who they are. She stresses there are many ways of marketing. Being successful at it means clarifying the message to be shared and finding a way to share that feels authentic.

Johnson lets several scenarios or situations tumble out as she talks about types of marketing. There's only so much time but so much information that she wants to impart.

Johnson has hired coaches herself. She found the assistance of a coach invaluable in helping her through transition times. None of them worked specifically with acupuncturists. It's the niche she wants to fill. She's been in a position to see the benefits of a good coach in her own business. She says that a coach can offer advice on where to focus marketing or business efforts. This advice can save a lot of wasted money and effort, making the money spent for coaching well worth it.

"You will be a success if you're persistent," Johnson says. Being persistent and passionate is the key to success. It's hard to be persistent when you are running out of money. Unfortunately, she doesn't have a solution to that. As a coach it's her goal to help practitioners not fall into this situation.

Johnson says that lots of acupuncturists aren't out talking to people and educating them about the medicine. In those cases, it can be hard to get people through the door. Practitioners need to be willing to do the work to find their place in the medicine. They need to go out and talk to people so they can connect with them and connect those potential patients with the medicine.

Since the interview Johnson has cut back on her coaching and has focused on her schooling at Duke University.

Hospital Internist

Sara Bublitz is a 2009 graduate from Oregon College of Oriental Medicine. At the time of the interview she maintained a private practice as well as working at the Mayo Clinic. Currently she is focused solely on her work at the Mayo Clinic.

Sara Bublitz: Collaboration is the Answer

Sara Bublitz is one of the newer graduates to be interviewed, having graduated in 2009 from Oregon College of Oriental Medicine. In addition to a successful practice, Sara works at the Mayo Clinic. Watching Sara talk about her struggles during that first year and building her practice, one is struck by the calmness of her large dark eyes. No doubt her patients find her a safe and healing presence.

Bublitz says that her first year of practice and transitioning out of school was hard. She struggled. She moved to Minnesota and was there on her own without a real network of other acupuncturists. She started in a small clinic that just didn't feel like it was the right fit. She saw two to eight patients a week. Feeling frustrated, she nearly gave up on the medicine because of how much she was struggling. Bublitz recalls, "I said to myself, I'm going to give it a year. I'm going to work my butt off for a year."

She spent that time networking, marketing and talking to people. At about eight months she connected with the clinic where she still practices. She went from maybe eight patients a week to sixteen. Bublitz says that jump was huge. "It gave me hope that I could do better."

Bublitz was willing to change her focus. Instead of remaining in the city, she was willing to go to the suburbs, broadening her criteria. She feels that's what she needed to do to be successful in her practice. She found a great partner, another acupuncturist who wanted to have a successful practice. Instead of working alone in the small clinic, she now had another person with which to collaborate. Bublitz joined an established clinic where the other practitioner needed to turn people away. "I think the difference was a collaborative effort, versus me doing it all on my own," Bublitz says.

Bublitz is very active on Facebook. She thinks that social media is one of the best ways to market herself. Sharing her love of acupuncture has been important to her success. A lot of acupuncturists are more introverted and aren't always good at social media. She was able to build up the Facebook business page. She wasn't afraid to inform people or ask them to tell others about it.

"I think the biggest key is educating people without an agenda," Bublitz says of her marketing efforts. She will inform people about their health without asking for something in return. Ultimately by educating people about what she does and what the medicine can do, people talk about her. She only posts one or two key topics on her business page so that people don't get tired of her posts. Sometimes she goes a few weeks between postings on her business page.

Bublitz always wanted to work in the hospital system. She had two knee surgeries in fourth and eighth grade and was left in a lot of pain. She wanted to go into medicine so that people had a different experience than what she had. She thought she might be a medical doctor or surgeon. Then she saw a lecture on acupuncture and that changed everything.

She got a degree in biology. After that she moved to Portland, Oregon. While attending OCOM she always had the vision of working in a hospital. She interviewed at four different hospitals before she got the job.

"I didn't see myself just working on my own in a single person practice," Bublitz says. Working with other people was important and it may be the reason that practicing on her own in the smaller clinic just didn't work out for her.

Hospital jobs are starting to open up. Minnesota has many hospitals that are hiring acupuncturists. Bublitz signed on to many different job websites so she'd be notified when hospitals had postings. She started sending out her resume and using those hospital interviews as learning experiences.

A lot of practitioners aren't searching, according to Bublitz. They don't know how to look, but most jobs are posted somewhere online. Bublitz says it was helpful to be in Minnesota where there is a demand for acupuncturists willing to work in a hospital.

"Mayo is so relevant and it's so progressive," Bublitz says. It validates her in everything that she's done. She loves that the hospital values acupuncture and that they see it as helping their patients. She loves her private practice but then goes to the hospital and the patients are all referred by their physicians. In the hospital setting, she sees spinal pain and lots of women's health. She was surprised to have the women's health referrals in the hospital. Physicians are seeing changes in the patients and are continuing to refer.

The chronic fatigue and fibromyalgia clinic wants the

acupuncturists in their department more frequently. They see their patients getting great results and the doctors there want more access. That means that Bublitz is giving more information to the department. She is also answering many questions from the Sports Medicine Clinic.

One of her tasks is to educate the doctors about what an acupuncturist does so that they understand. It's slower than she thought it would be. Bublitz thinks this could be huge in five to ten years.

Her hospital is insurance based for the most part. Medicare doesn't pay for acupuncture and lots of patients are on Medicare. The hospital bills insurance as much as they can. If the insurance won't cover it, the patients must pay. Bublitz sees up to eleven patients a day and one to three of them are new. Practitioners can be booked out for three months.

Bublitz gives the following simple advice to new acupuncturists, "Don't give up." She was ready to give up. She was broke and feeling like a failure. She worked three jobs. She realized she needed to reach out and connect more. She looked at the community and looked for what else she could do. She needed to be an extroverted business person and not an introverted acupuncturist.

Bublitz networked with other successful practitioners and also different business venues to get her name out there. Referrals will start coming in, Bublitz says, but it takes time. Once that happens, it starts feeling easy. But those first two years can be hard.

Bublitz feels that having a specialty helped her in private practice. She focuses on women's health and pain and then started learning everything she could on fertility. While she has a niche in private practice, she sees a little of everything in the hospital.

Bublitz says the key was deciding what success means.

She likes to see 12 to 15 people a day. The questions she would ask a new practitioner are:

- How much do you want to work?
- How much do you want to make?
- What types of patients do you want to see?

Then make that happen.

Bublitz focused on what she wanted in five years. Two years in she didn't think she could make her goals, but she stayed focused on her dream and kept working. Bublitz says it took vision, action, and passion for the medicine.

She gets excited about the patients and cares greatly about them. Bublitz isn't afraid to show her personality. At the same time, she's not afraid to charge people for her time. She also thinks about what makes it the easiest for the patient to come in and schedule. She considers what makes the patient comfortable in the treatment room. "Patients want to know what the plan is," Bublitz says. She gives them a specific treatment plan so patients know how often they will need to come in and can schedule accordingly.

"At the beginning I was very flexible with my time," Bublitz says. She thinks that in the beginning, practitioners should see people whenever they can, but as their business grows, then they can scale back to the hours that work for them.

Bublitz's next goal is to work with more professional athletes and at the specialty clinics at Mayo. Within the hospital, she would like to have acupuncturists in different niches. She'd like to be in one of those niches. "We're even better practitioners when we're able to hone in on a specialization." Bublitz would love to work a couple of days a week working with athletes and then a couple of others working in the IVF clinic.

You can contact Sara through her Facebook page <u>Sara Bublitz, Licensed Acupuncturist</u>. She is happy to respond to any questions. Since the interview, Bublitz has begun working full time at the Mayo Clinic and no longer works at her private practice.

PART III

The Educator

effrey Grossman has been in practice since 1997. Before that he was a graphic designer. His business, *Acupuncture Media Works* is one of the only businesses with marketing tools focused just for acupuncturists. In addition to print materials, Grossman has grown his business to include websites. If that's not enough, he has continued to practice acupuncture.

Education goes beyond just teaching the general public and offering information. Ryan Bemis is also an educator. He's a community acupuncturist. In addition to running a busy low cost clinic, he trains others in NADA protocols and educates allied healthcare providers about what acupuncture can do. He's building a community and in doing so he's educating far beyond his own clinic.

Education does indeed come in many different shapes and sizes.

The Marketeer

Jeffrey Grossman is a 1997 graduate of the New England School of Acupuncture. He currently has a private practice and runs Acupuncture Media Works and AcuPerfect Websites.

Jeffrey Grossman, LAc:
Acupuncture Can Change
the World

It's difficult not to be enthusiastic about acupuncture when talking to Jeffrey Grossman. He keeps smiling, talking about the medicine, completely animated, motioning with his hands to make a point. His beard laced with gray is the only sign that he's not fresh out of acupuncture school. Grossman is an acupuncturist as well as the owner of *Acupuncture Media Works* and *AcuPerfect Websites.*

"My degree was in communications and advertising... way back when... I was there when the very first Macintosh came out into the design room..." Grossman says when asked about his life before acupuncture school. During the time he worked in graphics and design, he read a lot of Native American healing and philosophies. He was the person who brought co-workers natural headache remedies.

Grossman and his cousin were planning to set up espresso carts, back before Starbucks. Grossman's contribution would be teas for stress reduction, emotional imbalance, and menstrual pain. Re-thinking the plan, he and his cousin decided this wasn't quite the business model for them. So that left him looking around for what he wanted to do. A couple of weeks later he woke with severe back pain. After visiting the doctor, he went to see an acupuncturist.

"...Like everyone does." Grossman smiles, almost embarrassed by how nearly cliché his story has become. He describes himself as being completely transformed. It's not an uncommon story. Someone has pain or illness and they visit an acupuncturist and are so inspired by the medicine that they end up going to school and studying the medicine.

The first year was really challenging, according to Grossman. "It's kind of disheartening." He goes on to describe being very excited about the diagnostic tools and wanting to work but not being sure how to get new patients.

"Health fairs stink if you are sitting there selling yourself," Grossman comments, speaking about his early marketing efforts. He did a lot of health fairs and talks. When he switched his perception to selling the medicine rather than himself, it helped him detach from the outcome so he could just share the power of the medicine, which increased his success.

In addition to changing the focus of his message, Grossman adds, "I did Toastmasters every Thursday for about a year and a half where I perfected my comfort about getting up in front of people and talking about acupuncture." There are thousands of Toastmasters clubs and it's very affordable. Grossman says it was one of the most invaluable things he did in his first year.

In Toastmasters, other professionals were willing to critique the way he talked about acupuncture so he could perfect how he communicated the power of the medicine.

Of course, as a side effect, many of the other people in the group came to try out acupuncture.

As Grossman expanded his marketing to flyers and brochures, other practitioners began asking him for something similar to help them market their practices. At the time, there weren't any marketing materials and tools for this industry. No one was filling this niche, other than Blue Poppy, but their information wasn't as user friendly and simple as Grossman wanted for his practice. *Acupuncture Media Works* really strives to help the potential patient understand the concepts of the medicine.

Grossman managed to get a mailing list of about 100 people on the west coast and sent out a nice flyer and four sample postcards. He also enclosed an order form with a call to act by a certain date. He got about a 40% response rate, meaning nearly 40% of the people responded and ordered from him. *Acupuncture Media Works* was born. He took that leap of faith that there was a need for his services.

Of course, Grossman made mistakes while building his business. If he didn't have a call to action when doing talks or health fairs, people might have enjoyed it but they didn't come in and see him.

To combat that, Grossman began offering free fifteen minute stress reduction treatments. He offered a limited number of these sessions to create an urgency. This allowed him to add value to his talks. It also allowed him to get people into his office where he could expand his educational efforts while letting curious people learn more about acupuncture in a safe environment.

"My marketing efforts really started paying off," Grossman says. In his stress reduction treatments, he'd do point zero and shen men. Having a call to action helped make those marketing efforts pay off.

Of course, he continues, it was really important for him that he sell the medicine rather than himself. "Acupuncture can transform the world, one person, a couple needles, at a time," Grossman says.

"My formula for success...has been offering the 20-20-2 technique." He offers a twenty minute session for either twenty dollars or free, depending upon the situation. During that treatment he does his two stress reduction points, point zero and shen men.

He also uses a very thorough report of findings. It explains what he found, what's wrong with the patient, how long the treatments will take and whether insurance covers it. "I usually suggest that I want to work with them for eight treatments and reevaluate." Most patients sign up for four or more treatments right after the report of findings.

This gets people on the books as far out as possible. Using the report of findings, helped him educate people and gets those same people to commit to longer term care.

Grossman is just getting back into practice again after a few years off, taking care of a small child. He's really excited about that. What inspires him is that he whole heartedly feels that acupuncture can change lives. The mini treatment helps people experience it, see his space, and get over any needle fears. There isn't any shortage of ideas for him to try. When he finds success with those ideas, *Acupuncture Media Works* lets him share those ideas with others.

"You really have to wear two hats: the hat of the business person and the hat of the healer..." Most practitioners want to just wear the healer's hat rather than both. Grossman wants to encourage people to embrace the idea of running a business successfully.

For Grossman it's about education, attracting patients,

informing them, inspiring them, and giving them good medicine. The tools for good medicine are there. The problem seems to be getting those patients in from day one. "You got to love it," Grossman says about marketing. "You can do that if you realize you are selling the profound effects and energy and experience of what acupuncture can offer. You can change lives."

For Grossman, the next steps include adding new features to *AcuPerfect Websites*. He's also going to be building a cash practice. He looks forward to coming up with new products that help practitioners build their own practices and embrace marketing, whether in print or online.

For people who want to learn more about Jeffrey Grossman and what he does, they can go to his website at **Acupuncture Media Works.com**.

The Community Trainer

Ryan Bemis, DOM is the director at Crossroads Community Supported Healthcare in New Mexico.

Ryan Bemis: Making
Acupuncture Accessible

A lot of acupuncturists talk about working for a non-profit or making their business a non-profit. Ryan Bemis acted on that idea. He is the director of Crossroads Community Supported Healthcare in New Mexico, a non-profit clinic. His mission is to make acupuncture accessible and affordable to people of all income levels.

Crossroads was once Bemis's clinic, where he was the owner/operator. In order to become a non-profit, he had to turn over the clinic to a board of directors. He is now the director of the clinic rather than the owner.

Crossroads offers low cost services. It provides trainings and cost effective techniques that can be taught to other healthcare providers. They also work with underserved groups in the area to help create and sustain their own community supported healthcare systems.

Bemis's road to acupuncture began while he was working at Hooper Detox in Portland, Oregon as a counselor. Hooper used acupuncture to treat alcohol and drug addictions. Bemis watched practitioners and students provide acupuncture in that setting. Oregon doesn't allow addiction counselors to use acupuncture, which meant if he wanted to use that tool, Bemis would have to study the medicine and become licensed.

The sliding scale clinic model became familiar to him when he used such a clinic for himself. He would never have been able to afford treatments without that sliding scale and he knew that that was a great way to help people afford their healthcare.

After acupuncture school, Bemis moved to New Mexico, where he's a DOM and can train people in the NADA protocol. He trains counselors and other allied healthcare professionals.

Although Bemis is a primary care provider, he doesn't incorporate it into his practice. Most practitioners in New Mexico don't. Bemis says he has a typical community acupuncture clinic. The big difference is that he provides NADA training to other professionals.

New Mexico makes it a bit challenging for acupuncturists to come work there. The license there requires a special test which is only offered twice a year. Additionally, the license is very expensive. It makes it hard for Bemis to get practitioners to come work at his clinic. "That's probably the biggest barrier to our clinic growing and expanding," Bemis says.

The first year of practice was difficult and challenging. It forced Bemis to reach out and ask for help. Prior to running his acupuncture clinic, he had had no business experience. He had a plan but not the experience to implement it. Bemis says he had never balanced his check book and suddenly he had a lot of responsibilities as far as accounting and book keeping.

Early on, Bemis's clinic started slowly. When the clinic

opened he saw maybe one patient a day. By the end of the year he was seeing about a hundred patients a week.

Bemis talks about making lots of mistakes. He had to rely a lot on mentors and other practitioners who ran community clinics in order to survive and grow his clinic. "I'm still on a really steep learning curve," Bemis says. "You just have to keep on getting up and keep going."

Bemis relied a lot on peer mentorship for support. His family was willing to help him with money to get him through that first year. He says he got a lot of acupuncture. He also credits staying connected. There weren't a lot of acupuncturists and no one doing group acupuncture in the area so he had to create a community for himself.

The community grew through the NADA trainings. Crossroads trained about one hundred and fifteen people to do NADA. The students were leading the board. At the time of the interview, Bemis was in his third year as part of that clinic.

"What most graduates need is just a job that they can step into," Bemis says. The ideal situation, he continues, is to work as an employee where the new acupuncturist can get experience and mentorship before setting up their own clinic. The great thing is that now there are more jobs in the field of acupuncture.

Bemis travels to Mexico once or twice a month. He doesn't operate a clinic there. He mostly trains and supervises practitioners. They're a big inspiration and a big part of what Bemis thinks of as his community. The travel helps him out of the daily grind. It also offers perspective. Bemis says that the challenges practitioners have in Mexico are harder than what he has in the United States.

Building community is the most rewarding aspect of the work Bemis does. Acupuncture is relational work, according to Bemis. Before he opened the clinic he didn't know many people in the area. Now, after training and treating so many people, he knows the community and he's part of it. He stresses that community is what holds things together. It's where you get support and engagement.

Bemis talks about being a young person starting a business like Crossroads. He had never tried being an entrepreneur but he wanted the clinic to thrive. He didn't want to make up what had to be done. He wanted to know what worked.

He became a member of People's Organization of Community Acupuncture and through that network he was able to join a peer mentorship program. They offer that both to people working in a community setting and for those who run a clinic. In addition, he works with NADA practitioners for mentorship and a local business group.

Of all the mentorship programs, POCAcoop has the most structured mentor program as well as online forums. POCAcoop focuses on one type of community acupuncture model. Bemis adapted several types of models to create his clinic in New Mexico.

Bemis talked to many people about their business models and adapted their ideas for what he envisioned. He looked at what clinics that worked were doing. Then he looked at clinics that weren't working. He analyzed what the clinics were doing differently.

Bemis also talks about having to be adaptive. The movement is very young so it's changing. That means he's always learning. Crossroads has provided over forty thousand treatments either through direct treatments or trainings and projects.

Making Crossroads sustainable over the long term is still a challenge. Over the next years Bemis says he's going to keep working on keeping it sustainable and making it thrive. There's still a long ways to go. He'd like to see the clinic become less dependent on him to keep it going.

Ryan Bemis can be contacted at **Crossroadsacupuncture.com**. There is a blog and information in both English and Spanish.

NADA's website is **acudetox.com**. POCA's website is **POCAcoop.com**.

PART IV

The Pioneer

As a growing profession there are many aspects that require blazing new trails. Diana Hermann is leading the way by creating new products that can be used in clinics. Becca Seitz has created a course on animal acupuncture and is dedicated to bringing acupuncture to animals. Matt Bauer is working on changing the entire perception of acupuncture.

Interviewing these three, one would think every acupuncturist is a trail blazer. And, of course, they are. Each new business is a new trail. Challenging policy or creating a product isn't for everyone and not everyone lives in a state that allows acupuncturists to treat animals, but every acupuncturist who runs a small business is a pioneer and can learn something from the unique challenges these three practitioners have faced in doing something really different.

Diana Hermann: Personal Contact and Building Relationships

Diana Hermann is a 1999 Oregon College of Oriental Medicine graduate, although she looks young enough to have graduated just within the last few years. Maybe she looks that young because she's designed skin care products based on Oriental Medicine principles? At any rate, Zi Zai Dermatology has a growing fan base with a variety of products that help patients as well as other practitioners who have often lacked access to topicals for patients with skin conditions.

"I do love what I do," Hermann says when asked about her products and doing acupuncture. The line of products is designed to treat specific dermatological conditions, eczema or psoriasis. Hermann started focusing on this because people with skin conditions tend to want to pull back from social interactions and display the psychological issues resulting from shame around their condition. Her products are designed to help them get back into the social aspect of their life.

Hermann only began creating products about six years ago, although she'd been out of school for years. Her initial year was spent close to her family where there were a lot of people who were willing to try acupuncture, thinking, "Now I can go to someone I trust." It was nice because of the connections. It was very different when she moved back to Colorado and started her business there.

Colorado wasn't new to Hermann. She'd been a student there, but she didn't have the wide network of friends and relatives to help her out. She joined several business networking groups and got to know a small handful of people well. They began sending people to her. From there, she was able to rely on word of mouth. "It was all building relationships on the personal level and having people trust me," Hermann says.

"My company got big by accident," Hermann laughs. It was always something she knew she would do someday. She was on vacation in Florida and got a terrible bacterial infection. She had an itchy rash that nothing was helping. Hermann decided to create something to help herself. Hermann's 'someday' had arrived.

Hermann began to experiment with ointments in her kitchen. Then she took classes on creating skin care products. She read whatever she could find and watched videos. She had some products that she knew were good but even then, she wasn't certain how to let people know about what she'd done.

On the advice of people around her, she started a blog. During the early days, Hermann discovered that she was allergic to propolis, which is a group of chemicals mixed in beeswax. After a lot of searching, she found one report where bee keepers got the same sort of rash on their hands. Hermann realized that was what was happening to her. She wrote up her information on her blog. Because there was no other information on that sort of rash, people found her business through that particular blog post. Then they would tell their friends about it.

Seeing a need, Hermann designed a lip balm that did not have beeswax. It remains her biggest selling product.

"If you're doing the same thing day in and day out, to me, that's boring," Hermann says. Her product line helped keep her interested in the medicine. It's the same herbs but she is using them in a different way. She says she loves making messes in her lab. She's learning more and taking new classes. That made the medicine fun because it was new again.

Hermann says, "You have to find the thing that you're interested in." It made the marketing easier for her, because she was passionate about it. She solved her own rash problem. In doing so, she solved a problem that many other people were having.

"Be you," Hermann continues. "Keep it fresh and keep it new." Don't put out the package you think people want to see but be who you are. Hermann talks about having images of her with the rash from when she used products with beeswax, calling it a "clown rash" online. There are also images of her with shingles which she took to illustrate her blog post on working with shingles.

"You can be afraid to make mistakes, and you're still going to make mistakes," Hermann says. She says everyone makes mistakes, so just learn from them. Hermann goes on to say that mistakes are one of her most effective teachers because then she knows what she shouldn't do.

"You can't be worried about failing because you'll never try," Hermann comments. Even in her product line she's had to work by trial and error. Sometimes products don't work for the condition she intended but are great for something else. Hermann calls her ability to adapt as being opened minded about what she's doing.

Hermann grew her business in steps. Initially, she worked her product line as if it would just be something to help her own patients, printing labels from her computer. She continues to do this with new products. For products she is ready to release to the world, she has professionally designed labels. True to her philosophy that all business is about relationships, Hermann found a logo maker and designer through a personal association in her town.

Certainly that design takes money. It's an investment in her business. Hermann didn't want to borrow money but she did take a bit from her parents to get her website and labels designed. When the business makes money she puts that money back into the business to develop the next product.

Hermann's product line has gotten large enough that she has hired someone to ship the products out. She has started letting others do the things she's not good at, like graphic design. She formulates and makes the products. She also does all the social media because she remains the face of her business.

Hermann says she doesn't have much competition because she started this company when she couldn't find what she needed for herself. She's not just another skin care company. Her products are based on Chinese Herbal Medicine and her products are designed for very specific skin conditions with a TCM diagnosis. Her market is more niche market than other skin care product producers and it fills a need.

In general, Hermann thinks people are now much more aware of acupuncture than when she graduated. Demand is greater and there is room for greater supply. It's not really about competition and more about doing what you do well.

Hermann plans to work on her dermatological

specialty. In 2015 she's going to study with a well-known specialist even though it requires traveling to London five times during the year. There's a need for acupuncturists who understand dermatological problems. Still, she is aware she needs to do some educating. The focus of her educational efforts will be dermatologists in her community, showing them what acupuncture can do to help them help their patients. It's about building relationships with other practitioners.

Hermann says that acupuncturists who are struggling need to remember why they went into the medicine in the first place. Hermann felt she got bogged down in the business aspects of her practice. It started suffering because she was really unhappy about her work.

Hermann said she had to find a way to make herself be happy to come to work. She recommends finding someone to do the work you really hate doing. Whether that task is cleaning, accounting, or insurance billing, get someone else to do the work you hate so you can do what you love. Hermann recognizes that that's a cost, but "the weight off your shoulders is worth it." When that's gone, practitioners have more energy for treating patients.

According to Hermann there are now so many more options for acupuncturists. It's easier to find places to work rather than being forced into being your own boss. It's much easier to outsource administrative tasks, like scheduling. As far as Hermann is concerned, this is great news for new practitioners.

For more information on Diana Hermann, LAc you can go to her website at **ZiZaiDermatology.com**.

The Product Creator

Diana Hermann graduated from Oregon College of Oriental Medicine in 1999. She practices in Fort Collins Colorado and runs Zi Zai Dermatology, which includes a clinic specializing in dermatology issues and a product line.

The Policy Changer

Matt Bauer, LAc began practicing acupuncture in 1986. He currently runs LaVerne Acupuncture and is president of the Acupuncture Now Foundation.

Matt Bauer: Senior Acupuncturist on Educating the World

M att Bauer is a name that isn't as familiar to people as it should be. He's written a lot about acupuncture and when you read his writing you get the expectation that he's this really outgoing, yang sort of person. Instead, he self describes himself as being very yin. That's evident in the video. He's articulate, and while he gestures, his hands are mostly near the bottom of the screen and he sits quietly looking like a Daoist Master. Of course, Daoism is where his interest in acupuncture developed.

Bauer's acupuncture journey started when he injured his back at seventeen. He'd dabbled in martial arts so he picked up a book on shiatsu. The book wasn't written for self-healing but for healing others. Still, interest wetted, Bauer went to a Whole Life Expo and saw Iona and Ron Teagarten who were talking about acupressure. The Teagartens had a school in Santa Monica where they were going to have a shiatsu master for a workshop. Bauer wanted to learn how to help his back so he went. There, he was just amazed with the level of bodywork, both the skill and technique, as well as with the technique of abdominal diagnosis.

He picked up a flyer at the workshop which advertised acupuncture. During this shiatsu course he learned a little more about Oriental medicine overall, not just the acupressure method. Bauer had a family member with thyroid issues so he called the acupuncturist's office. The assistant said acupuncture could help.

Both Bauer and his family member began having acupuncture. Six weeks later the family member with the thyroid issue had a normal thyroid scan. The doctor was certain it had nothing to do with the acupuncture and herbs but Bauer was convinced it did.

He began studying Daoist philosophy very seriously with Master Nghi. He didn't think he would do the medicine. He just wanted to study the philosophy which is what he did for about five years. At around that time he was considering a career change. "I was thinking about acupuncture but there weren't any schools near me or hours that worked for me," Bauer says.

Then he heard about a school which had opened close to him. "I was sitting in class the next day."

Upon finishing school Bauer moved to a new neighborhood and he opened his office. "We didn't even discuss practice management in my school," Bauer says. He leased an office to see what would happen. He was supposed to have a partner in the office but she pulled out at the last minute. Looking back, he believes that being thrown into the deep end was a good thing. He was at the office at least 40 or 50 hours a week. If there wasn't a patient, he was working on trying to figure out how to get people into the office. He had a wife and two children to support.

"If you have a plan and work the plan, I believe within two to three years most practitioners should be grossing at least $100,000 a year," Bauer says. He writes about this in his book **Making Acupuncture Pay**. Bauer acknowledges that starting out is scary and takes some initial investment but it can be done.

A lot of acupuncturists rent a room rather than building a business from scratch. While there are advantages in terms of costs, there are disadvantages too. You're trying to market yourself under the wing of someone else's business.

While there were many struggles in the first year, about eighteen months into it Bauer was able to support his family. They were living very modestly but they could pay bills and put a little bit away. Into his third year, he was still working the office totally on his own. He had a goal to clear $1,000 each week. He'd feel very accomplished when he did that. Then he'd remember he had to do that each and every week as the money built up.

"As you build that patient base it actually gets easier and easier," Bauer says. By year four, he didn't have to do any marketing any more. It was all word of mouth.

Bauer says it takes eighteen months to three years to get a business off the ground and thinks that students aren't given those numbers and that reality. Not many acupuncturists understand that they will have really lean years and more investments in their own offices before they can start making any money.

New practitioners don't have a clear picture of what it takes to build a successful practice. They think that they can do it on half time hours. But the more they limit their accessibility the harder it is for people to get to them. Bauer isn't speaking about hours of operation, but also the office being accessible. Can people get there? Are the fees accessible? Does the practice accept insurance? What about credit cards?

Public awareness is a big issue. When Bauer was in his second year of practice, he was contacted by the California Acupuncture Association. He knew about them because they had a bill they wanted passed so that acupuncture would be covered by insurance. When they contacted him about working with them, Bauer assumed that one of the top items would be to connect with the public and explain what acupuncture was about. He was hoping they'd make brochures. At that time there wasn't a single professionally published brochure. But the group didn't want to do that.

Bauer took the initiative and talked to a media consultant and she was willing to do training on how to educate the public. Again, the board wasn't interested. The leadership of many organizations say they want to increase public awareness but are always busy doing other things. Bauer acknowledges that those other things are important too.

Bauer uses the following analogy to illustrate his point: "You have a patient that comes to you with multiple... health issues, and you need to learn to kind of triage...Yes, we're holistic. We want to treat a lot of things at once. But you don't really treat a whole lot of things at once totally equally." That's the way he's looked at the growth of the profession.

There had to be legislation to make the practice of acupuncture legal. The accreditation process for colleges and curriculum had to be formed. Then there was the need for national standards. Acupuncturists got most of those taken care of over twenty years ago but the profession still isn't working on raising awareness of the efficacy of acupuncture.

Bauer knows that educating the public is something

every practitioner wants. He kept going to the leadership of acupuncture organizations about the issue. Too often the leadership was too unorganized to get the job done.

It was for this reason that Bauer decided to found the *Acupuncture Now Foundation* which can be accessed online at **AcupunctureNowFoundation.org**. It's just getting started but the mission is to educate the public, law makers, and health care professionals about acupuncture.

Bauer envisioned that such an organization would eventually be international. He sees the same problems happening everywhere in the west. One major problem is the lack of effective leadership. There is also a lot of divisiveness over issues like training standards.

When it comes to educating the public, most acupuncturists believe it is important. It has the potential to get practitioners to rally around it. If you start seeing positive news reports about acupuncture and oriental medicine, acupuncturists will know that someone is doing something. This kind of education will put patients in the waiting rooms of acupuncturists. Bauer says that kind of publicity could double the number of patients seeking out acupuncturists within five years if there was a well-funded public education campaign.

To create such a campaign and help it thrive, there needs to be an organization that earns the reputation that has the authoritative and unbiased information on acupuncture.

For the individual practitioner, "It's not just about marketing," Bauer says. You need two great skills. Practitioners need to get patients in their door. Then they need to go out that door happy with the results. Of those two, the second one is the most important.

Bauer leaves writing about marketing until the final

chapters of his book **Making Acupuncture Pay** because he is so certain that a successful practice isn't about marketing. He says acupuncturists need to be both good clinicians and marketers.

Bauer is now donating all proceeds of **Making Acupuncture Pay** to the *Acupuncture Now Foundation*. He says he can give advice on how practitioners can market themselves but what needs to happen is getting a national campaign going. Acupuncturists need to get penetration on a national level. Bauer wants to zero in on an easy to understand message like the fact that acupuncture helps the body to heal itself.

Individual practitioners can be echoing that message with their own personal touch within their market. The idea is that acupuncturists need more collective education of the public and collective marketing. He's also offering continuing education courses and all the proceeds are going towards the *Acupuncture Now Foundation* to fund this campaign.

"It's a daunting thing," Bauer says. The ideas are taking off faster than he expected.

Acupuncture represents the greatest natural healing knowledge that's ever been developed. There's virtually no field of medicine in which acupuncture can't be a contribution, whether it's a primary or supportive therapy. It's natural. Acupuncture can produce results. If people understood what acupuncturists can do, everyone would want it. Acupuncturists could all make a living.

Bauer has been in the profession twenty-nine years. He's looking to build an online publication that lets people know what colleagues are doing in other countries. The profession was at its lowest point in the first half of the twentieth century but now it's at its highest point.

You can find *Acupuncture Now* on the Facebook page **Acupuncturists for Acupuncture Now.** He wanted to build a communicative venue so that people know what others are doing and to get their feedback on what's happening. Contact Bauer through the website **AcupunctureNowFoundation.com**.

The Visionary

Becca Seitz, LAc is a 2006 graduate and the owner of Thrive Acupuncture in Portland, Oregon. She is also the president of the International Academy of Animal Acupuncture.

Becca Seitz: For the love of Animals

B ecca Seitz sits in on a comfortable looking piece of furniture with many recognizable acupuncture books on the shelves behind her. She smiles easily and speaks knowledgably about the practice of acupuncture on animals. Seitz lives and practices in Oregon where her license allows her to practice on animals as well as people. That's not true of all states.

Seitz was originally planning on studying veterinary medicine when her acupuncturist talked about animal acupuncture. "A light bulb went off," Seitz said. She intended to go to both vet school and acupuncture school. She got into school for acupuncture first and learned that allied health professionals in the state of Oregon were allowed to treat animals with a referral from a veterinarian.

Due to the staggering cost of going to veterinary school as well as the fact that Seitz was particularly drawn to practicing acupuncture, she decided that she would use the knowledge she had gained and work with veterinarians to help animals using the medicine.

Seitz worked at the Oregon Humane Society before

she went to acupuncture school. During school, she worked in a veterinary clinic where the veterinarian practiced animal acupuncture. The veterinarian would ask her what channel she had learned in school that week and would then teach her the point locations on the animals.

Aside from the hands on training, there wasn't a lot of information available to practitioners who want to learn to treat pets. Seitz is working with Gene Bruno to assemble a training course for acupuncturists to learn animal acupuncture. She says there is some information from the veterinary world, but it's not always accurate. Seitz and Bruno are working to fix that.

Seitz works part time as an acupuncturist, treating human patients. Her schedule is constrained because she has small children. She became pregnant right after graduating and she remains the primary caregiver for her family. Seitz says she was able to pay the bills with her clinic but didn't have any money left over. Her husband was a 'fantastic cheerleader.' He reminded her that the struggle of opening a practice was short term in the grand scheme of things.

"For the amount of hours I am putting in, um...I am bringing home money now..." Seitz says. At some point she would like to expand her practice, particularly as her children get older.

While many acupuncturists struggle with the decision to take insurance, it's not an option for pets, although some pet insurance companies are beginning to cover acupuncture. Policy holders would have to be clear about whether it would cover only a veterinarian or an allied healthcare professional.

Seitz has worked at a couple of different veterinary offices and those doctors refer to her now. Most of her pet patients come because their owners are her patients. After seeing results on themselves they want to offer that to their pet too. Often Seitz doesn't have a relationship with the veterinarian so the owner has to ask for a referral.

There are many advantages to working with pets. Seitz gets to experience first-hand that there is no placebo effect. According to Seitz, her favorite part is, "They get better so quickly... about half the time of their human counterparts." Sometimes it's hard to shift back and forth between pet and human. It takes so much longer to heal in a human.

As the owner of two cats, Seitz really enjoys working with felines. Owners don't always trust their cats to remain calm during a treatment but often they are easier to treat than dogs. One of Seitz's favorites was a Manx with a short tail. Manx cats often have problems along the spine. Some nerves will be missing or compressed. This particular cat had long standing constipation. Seitz did electro-acupuncture around the area that was malformed and prescribed some herbs. The cat was no longer constipated and has not had to have more treatment.

Seitz has a long history of working with small animals, which is the focus of her practice, so she doesn't worry about bites and scratches. She's well aware of when an animal is uncomfortable with the situation. Most animals are okay with the treatment. There are rare cases that the animal doesn't want to be touched, such as a dog that had arthritis.

Small animal acupuncture isn't limited to cats and dogs. "I treated an iguana once," Seitz says. "It was a really cool experience."

Seitz did face some questions when she said she wanted to work on animals. Teachers didn't always understand her desire. Veterinarians may be hesitant about non-veterinarians working on animals. It's one reason Seitz is working on training acupuncturists about small animal anatomy.

Many people have great ideas for bringing acupuncture to markets that are not well-served. There are always naysayers. "Be more stubborn than they are," Seitz says. She advises taking the steps to do what you really love. So long as you're following the law, no one can tell you it can't be done.

Seitz and Bruno graduated the first class from the International Academy of Animal Acupuncture in March 2015. They've created a board certification for animal acupuncture as well. Currently there are five fellows. Seitz is getting ready to do the second round of classes in November.

For those interested in studying to treat animals, they can find out about their state's regulations on the AVMA site, **avma.org/Advocacy/StateAndLo-cal/Pages/sr-cavm-exemptions.aspx**. Seitz cautions that while this is the best listing out there, it is not one hundred percent accurate and it's a good idea to double check with the state in question.

The course that Seitz teaches can be found at the *International Academy of Animal Acupuncture* **Animal-AcupunctureAcademy.com**. Additionally the Maryland University of Integrative Health has classes. Interested students can also check out **AnimalAcupunctureBoard-.org** for more information about the certification.

Seitz can be contacted at her website **Thrive.org**.

PART V

Moving Beyond the Day to Day Needling

Both practitioners in the next section have worked through some business closing issues. They bring great insight into moving on, either to a new location or to another facet of life.

Kim Knight retired and moved on to another business. It's true that not everyone wants to continue practicing the medicine their entire life. Sometimes people find that they can be more helpful to the profession by doing something else. Kim has set up another business that allows her more flexibility and freedom to travel.

While Christina LeBoeuf is still actively practicing, she made a major life change and moved hundreds of miles from her first practice. Before doing so, she sold that practice, which is an act that more practitioners are thinking about doing as they age and get ready to retire. LeBoeuf has some great insights into what she saw as important in selling her practice and what she hoped to offer the buyer.

Both of these practitioners have information that can be helpful to those making the transition from active practitioner to retirement.

The Career Changer

Kim Knight is a 2007 graduate of Oregon College of Oriental Medicine and is owner of Acubiller Alchemy Credentialing.

Kim Knight: Experimentation and Change

Kim Knight looks very calm. She's the sort of person you can rely on. She knows what she's talking about. Knight's background includes a lot of widely varied experience. She clearly values being interested in her work and following wherever her path might lead her.

Knight was working with a home birth midwife in Montana when she discovered acupuncture. She attended a difficult birth and the mom had an acupuncturist. The acupuncturist was helping with the stuck baby.

"In my memory I remember it [the baby] flying out," Knight laughs. She was intrigued and wanted to know how that was possible. Acupuncture seemed almost magical.

Knight moved to Portland and considered studying naturopathic medicine at National College of Naturopathic Medicine but ended up at the Oregon College of Oriental Medicine instead.

Upon graduation, Knight knew she didn't want to join another practice or be hired on as a contractor. She knew she was a great employee but she didn't enjoy working for someone else. Unlike many new practitioners, Knight was excited about starting her own business.

"I learned a lot. I enjoyed the process," Knight says of her first year. She liked trying new things to see if they worked. Her practice grew consistently and steadily but not as fast as she would have liked. Building a new business was a challenge on a daily basis.

Knight believed in the idea that acupuncture had something to offer so she kept meeting her challenges. She found some of her early patients pushed her clinical skills, despite having had excellent training in the student clinic. It did occur to her that she could make more money doing something else. However, the idea of being part of a community and wanting to see that community grow kept her working at the medicine.

"Don't stress it," Knight recommends to new graduates. "It's called a practice for a reason."

It takes time to get good at treating and having the conversations with patients that need to happen. An acupuncturist needs to have a plan for working with patients. They need to test out the plan, seeing what works. Finally, they need to assess what doesn't work and try alternatives. Business is about continuing to do that. It's clear that Knight likes to follow a process even when she's experimenting.

"Sit down and think about what you want…a lot of people are struggling…are trying to hold on and spending a lot of energy on a part of their practice they don't even like," Knight says. Some don't like insurance billing, so maybe they give that up or hire someone to take on that task. Others might be treating a patient population they aren't that interested in.

For Knight, metrics are important. Even in the way she talks about implementing a plan, she talks about testing and refining the plan to learn what works. She measures the changes the plan brings and advises others to do so as well. It doesn't have to be in a formal spreadsheet. Maybe it's just a chart on the wall. Whatever it is, it should be something that allows the practitioner to track what works. Sometimes a metric doesn't seem useful when it's first tracked but it measures information that becomes useful later.

During the course of her years as an acupuncturist, Knight found a specialty. Her experience was that being a niche practitioner was very useful. People like focus. When someone talks about their niche, they're excited and excited about working with that person. The conversation becomes positive and educational for the patient. There's a clear path to the conversation and it's about whether or not the practitioner can help the patient.

It was after finding her niche that Knight became quite successful. That made her start thinking about change. "The goal was originally…make my work smaller spaces in time and make more money." That was difficult for her to manage. She didn't like having multiple patients each hour. Instead, she worked her schedule down to fewer work days each week and raised the quality of the patients she saw.

During this time Knight, along with her business partner Eliza, saw a real need for a hard- working, accurate, and ethical biller in town and rushed to start that business. Managing credentialing and Kim's business, *Alchemy Credentialing*, flowed naturally from *Acubiller*. After some market research and the realization that there was no one out there to support acupuncturists with credentialing, she went out on her own with the fully formed credentialing business, *Alchemy Credentialing*.

"I did love my practice," Knight says. She says that considering leaving her acupuncture business was harder than any of the other career changes she'd made. She spent a month of seriously contemplating whether she wanted to make that leap. Normally, Knight says, she makes those kinds of changes quickly because she's bored, but this was a bigger decision.

Acubiller helps people bill insurance and *Alchemy Credentialing* helps credential providers. "My life's awesome," Knight laughs when asked about work life balance. She has quality time with her business partner over at *Acubiller* and is able to shut things off at five o'clock

. She can work on credentialing wherever she is so long as there's a good internet connection.

Knight is into productivity and makes sure that work doesn't overwhelm her. She works ahead on slow days so that she doesn't have a twelve hour day later in the week. For her, it's about having good boundaries.

Currently Knight is building a partnership with Portland Therapy Center. She expects to continue to grow the credentialing business and is considering when she'll be able to take on a full time employee. As the business grows, she'll have more time to travel. After all, one reason she started these businesses to help other practitioners was so that she could travel. Knight says she probably has at least another five years before she gets bored with her current work.

Kim Knight can be found at **AlchemyCredentialing.com**.

The Practice Seller

Christina LeBoeuf graduated from the Atlantic Institute of Oriental Medicine. She currently practices at Carolina Holistic Health, after having built and sold a successful practice in another state.

Christina LeBoeuf: On Selling a Practice

O n the Facebook group, *Acupuncture Business Academy*, there are often questions about buying and selling a practice. Having already done so herself, Christina LeBoeuf, LAc is more than happy to share her knowledge of the process. In the interview Christina is equally helpful. Her large, lovely eyes draw you in and she speaks calmly and intelligently.

"I was very interested in natural medicine… my entire life," LeBoeuf says. Her main interest in the medicine came through herb therapy.

"I had a busy practice that I really enjoyed," LeBoeuf says. She says it kept her busy about sixty hours a week. It was in her hometown, which she liked. However, she had always wanted to live somewhere warm. She went to school in Fort Lauderdale which was warmer than she wanted. Once her practice in upstate New York was flourishing and she felt comfortable selling it to someone, she put it up for sale and decided to move south.

LeBoeuf says she built the practice for about seven years. When she considered moving, she knew she couldn't just let the practice go like so many practitioners do. Her patients needed care and there weren't any other options closer than an hour's drive. That meant that even if she had wanted to just leave, she didn't feel she could.

After doing her research, LeBoeuf went about marketing her practice. She let potential buyers know it was a very busy practice and that the area was rural. It was also very cold in the winter. She had several inquiries but only one of them stood out and that was the person who purchased the practice from her. LeBoeuf says that she spent about two months coaching the new practitioner in person and over the phone so that they settled in well with the patients.

"It is important to pick a person that will take over your practice that you trust to do a good job on behalf of your patients, and practices a similar style of acupuncture. I expect a lot. I expected the new person to be very intelligent, dedicated, willing to learn my techniques and the technologies I incorporated into my practice. [They had to be] caring, a great listener, willing to continue promoting the practice, and have a desire to continue to improve their skills. My practice is very successful and my community loves me so it was important to find someone to take over who was a lot like me or my patients would not continue care," LeBoeuf said.

Once she decided to sell, LeBoeuf did her research. She asked a lot of questions of a lot of people. She asked on Facebook groups, which she said were really helpful. Because her practice included the building, she had the 160 year old Victorian house on a half an acre of land appraised several times.

She looked at her finances annually so that she could show potential buyers that the business was still growing. She researched fair market value on the contents of the business, spending a lot of time on Craigslist and EBay. LeBoeuf says it helped that she was selling more than just the client list. She was selling the practice space, not just a lease. The building included an apartment above the clinic as well as an herb store that was attached to the clinic. That meant it was a good value for the buyer, even if patient load dropped off because the business had changed hands.

After the video interview, LeBoeuf talked a little more and answered a few other questions about how the buyer financed the purchase. She helped the buyer with financing. He made a small down payment and is paying her in increments until he can get a bank loan, at which point she will be paid in full and he will carry a mortgage on the property.

LeBoeuf says, "The person taking over was basically just stepping into my life." Everything was already set up and ready to go. It took about six months to sell.

The new business was rough to start over. She was used to seeing many patients a day but now had many fewer patients. Still, she knew she'd done it before and she felt confident she could build a practice again.

There are plenty of people in need of acupuncture. Acupuncturists just need to get out there and find them. LeBoeuf says that ninety percent of the people she meets have no idea what acupuncture can do for them. She lets them know that she'll be there when they need her. She hands out information and does education.

"It'll build, it always does," LeBoeuf says. The more people practitioners talk to the more people will come see them. She says everyone should get visible in their community.

If someone is looking to purchase a practice, they want to see that the practice is continuing to grow. That was the main factor in allowing LeBoeuf to feel good about selling her practice to someone else. Potential purchasers should look at tax returns for at least the past three years, five if the owner is comfortable providing them.

If the practitioner owns property that's important and adds value. In LeBoeuf's case she owned all the contents of the building as well as the building and the land. LeBoeuf says, "If someone was interested in purchasing a practice with no actual property other than patient files and a couple treatment tables, I would be cautious. I would ask to meet the landlord to discuss the terms. I would want to meet any other people in the building and others close by to talk about the area (safety, traffic, quality of building upkeep, ability to sublet, recent or near future development to the area, etc.). They [the seller] are basically selling their good name and it is common for 1/3 or more of the current patients to not continue care with the new practitioner....will the new person be able to pay the rent and afford to live? Does the seller have connections to help the buyer attract new patients?"

During the two months that LeBoeuf worked with her buyer, she not only introduced them to how she did things, she introduced them to her contacts within the community, which would allow the new person to continue to grow the practice. She was available by phone even after she left to ensure that the patients noticed the transition as little as possible.

For those thinking of purchasing a practice, don't be shy around the money conversation. You need something tangible to see what you're getting.

For LeBoeuf, she intends to build up her practice and stay where she is. She really likes South Carolina. She would love to build a beautiful integrated wellness center.

You can contact Christina at **carolinaholis-tichealthllc.com.**

Editor's note: Acupuncturists interested in buying or selling their practices may find further information at the **PractitionersJourney.com** in an article called how to value a practice. There are also professionals out there to help people value a practice and help with listings.

Afterword

I'd like to thank each and every practitioner who agreed to be interviewed for this book. I hope that all readers find something helpful within the summaries of those interviews or in the interviews themselves.

Acupuncture is a growing field and it's rapidly changing. Practitioners have a lot to keep up with even while they are still learning the medicine and how to run a business. There are more opportunities than ever to join a practice rather than start on one's own. While many students coming out of school don't feel that the salary is enough to let them pay their student loans and have a life, fifteen years ago finding employment as an acupuncturist, rather than starting one's own practice, was far more difficult.

Each of these practitioners has a successful practice. Each of them is moving beyond the success of their practice, whether that's working to grow the practice further, deciding to focus on a niche, or creating a product line. There are hundreds of acupuncturists out there all doing something similar. There are always opportunities for new practitioners to become successful.

Untold Stories has its own website where you can find the original, raw video feeds of each of these interviews. Go to **Untold.LilacPointPress.com**. The password to each of the interviews is Untold2015 (exactly as written). The summarization for the book does not detail all the information each practitioner gave. Writing question and answer responses make for dull reading and this is a book that is meant to be readable. I encourage you to watch the interviews of those practitioners you were particularly interested in.

About the Authors

Bonnie Koenig, LAc

Bonnie Koenig, LAc graduated from Oregon College of Oriental Medicine in 1999. She practiced in Vancouver, WA and then in North Bend, WA for over a dozen years before moving again and deciding to retire to write books.

Bonnie wrote the popular **Websites for Acupuncturists** book before beginning the **Untold** project. She blogs about business matters for acupuncturists as well as writing articles for *Acupuncture Today*. She assists in moderating the popular Facebook group, Acupuncture Business Academy, started by classmate Lisa Hanfileti, LAc.

In addition to writing about acupuncture, Bonnie also writes fiction as Bonnie Elizabeth. You can find her at BonnieKoenigLAc.com or at MyBigFatOrangeCat.com.

Jason Stein, LAc

Jason Stein, MOM, LAc earned his BS in psychology at Arizona State University in 1993 and his master's degree in Oriental medicine from the International Institute of Chinese Medicine in Albuquerque, NM in 1998. He established the first integrative medicine program in a Western hospital setting in New Mexico. He is a professional certified coach and teaches Mindfulness and Stress Resilience classes with Providence Health Systems.

You can find him at http://JasonStein.com.

Also by Bonnie Koenig, LAc

10 Myths about Acupuncture

Websites for Acupuncturists

Points to Ponder for the Acupuncturist in Business

Writing for Acupuncturists